# Health & Wealth Is Always Green

## How I Went From Elderly Care To The Cannabis Industry

Donnie P.

Donnie P.

# Contents

# Dedication

I dedicate this book with all praise and honor to the Creator of the Universe. The One who gave me life by fire, and now I live.

# Acknowledgments

This book is dedicated to my brother Omar; we make a great 1,2 combination. I have loved you ever since we grew up together, which benefits us as men. Also, to the great team we have had with our long-term care businesses and our dispensary team and family. One last note: I want to acknowledge the services and appreciation of the late Dr. Karl Haydel Sr. for our business. He was the only Doctor who came to our grand opening and welcomed us to the Houma region with open arms and to the great people of our region. We Love You!!!

# About the Author

Donnie P., an entrepreneur and native of Jeanerette, Louisiana, realized early in his professional business career that he was equipped with the necessary drive and determination that would allow him to start businesses—from the ground up—without any money.

With over 20 years of experience today, Donnie P. is guided by his unwavering faith in the Creator and desire to develop business platforms that will uplift others. Donnie P. is the founder and CEO of OSD Group, LLC, a cannabis dispensary owner/partner of Greenleaf Dispensary in Houma, Louisiana, The Still and Tubman Foundation, his non-profit foundation, and Blastoff Business Coaching. He launched A Caring Home Services' national franchise rollout in the middle of 2012. In August of 2013, he sold his first of many franchises to Karl and Beverley Stephens, LLC, out of Nashville, Tennessee. A Caring Franchise was sold in 2019

In 2014, Donnie P. Authored his first business book titled "How to Catch a Mouse with No Cheese," written for people who have been in business for up to a year or are interested in starting a business but do not have money. It discusses five life-changing principles that will help you succeed. Each principle has its basis for preparing you to grow your business with no money.

Since the launching of Donnie P.'s book "How to Catch a Mouse with No Cheese," it has been sold worldwide in the following Countries: the United States of America, Germany, New Zealand, France, India, Canada, and Great Britain. To learn more about Donnie P., go to his website at **www.donniepofficial.com**

# Chapter 1

As I stand in front of the mirror in one of the most expensive suits, with staff to look after me and a successful business in the Cannabis industry, I see the little version of Donnie (myself) in the mirror.

In his childhood, little Donnie is wearing an average suit, posing in front of the mirror. Many things had to go my way for me to reach where I am today. That doesn't necessarily mean things and events had to go in my favor but against my wishes too.

Every little to major success or any setback I faced throughout my journey had to be precisely the way they went because these all things shaped my life journey up till now. All the small, significant, and random events made a string of pebbles that turned into a beautiful bracelet, and this is how I see my life.

My journey toward becoming a successful entrepreneur started in a small country town in Louisiana. I came from a family that was a mix of entrepreneurs and educators; both my parents were educators at first.

In my infant to early kid years, I grew up in a salon that my grandmother owned. She was an epitome of iron lady in every sense—a very successful entrepreneur in her own way. And this was when the term "entrepreneur" was not popular like today.

I spent a lot of time in my grandmother's salon, which had a mix of vintage and classy vibes. It became like that as she didn't have the means to upgrade it to a clean, slick, flashy look. However, the equipment and the furniture were very much functional and did their job perfectly. Because of this, I was exposed to the insight of running a business early in my life. I learned both the phenomenon:

How a business is managed

How a business should be managed

Nothing beats the experience of seeing something firsthand. No matter how much we learn from books, the internet, and classrooms, it all comes down to practical experience in terms of business. How much one has seen firsthand in order to run a business comes first; whether successful or not is the question for later. To be honest, nothing or no one can teach you what you learn while eventually running your own business.

My grandmother's family had owned two salons over time. They knew how to grow and expand the business, which is another thing I learned naturally from them. Even one of the salons also had a kitchen, which was used for meal orders, adding another element to their enterprise. With all this, her family owned multiple properties in the city over time, which taught me another lesson—how to diversify a business.

Most of the small business persons or entrepreneurs I know and have seen, and you might have seen, remain in one place or low-key in their lifetime. They are usually popular and successful in their respective communities and areas and build a great reputation through word of mouth over time. However, they never scale or grow.

Maybe they don't know how to do it, or they don't want to risk doing it. They remain comfortable on their small scale, but the business climate doesn't remain the same. Things happen, and the economy changes; in short, life happens, so these businesses don't become the source of generational wealth in any way. Their profit entirely depends on the effort and time they put into it. They never become self-sustainable.

The exposure to other businesses, like running a kitchen and investing in real estate options, gave my grandmother and her family the freedom to grow. They just then didn't depend on a single source of income; again, this all comes with risk. One has to take the initial risk of doing something like that. Nothing in life is guaranteed, let alone in businesses, but one must trust his intuition and business acumen to do something like this. Without going into detail, many factors and techniques are involved in doing something like this. I'll discuss all of these things in the upcoming chapters.

These were among the many things I learned unknowingly, and I later discovered their roots. Also, I learned many things with full awareness and desire. One of my earliest memories is when my sister, my cousin, and I used to close the salon at night with my grandmother. One thing I noticed was that she always carried her gun with her. I guess it was the idea of business safety and insurance in those times. She did not keep it to harm anyone but to defend herself and her business in unusual or threatening circumstances.

After closing the salon, we used to go home with her. When we would reach home, one of the first things she would do was count the money; every day in and day out, she would do this. I didn't think much of it, but there is a reason I remember this detail to this day. It was evident how much she was invested in her business. I don't mean financially but physically and mentally. She dedicated her time and effort, and that too with consistent discipline.

Besides all the technical things that make a business successful, which I will discuss later, the heart of any business lies in these things. These are the qualities that make someone a successful and effective entrepreneur. Seeing this every night taught me a lot, and very consciously, from my early years, I tried to develop these qualities in myself too.

***

Besides the Creator, my parents were the people who impacted my life largely. They were tough, intelligent, and loving. They both were educators, so I grew up in a household that stressed was big on education. Without education, I would not get any privilege or my way into anything. It was like a duty that I did, and it was indeed very helpful in many ways, especially for my future. Another thing they stressed in our household was self-discipline, and they didn't compromise it at all.

It was not one of those things my parents just instructed us in conversations; they lived by every bit of the values they taught us. They were role models for us to follow these things.

One instance I remember that articulates these qualities involves my father. I was around 8 years old when my dad used to run Bingo's. The whole concept of running something like this required dedication, self-discipline, and patience.

After doing his regular job during the weekdays with dedication, he would occupy his weekends too. He used to wake me up early in the mornings on weekends, and the journey of organizing a Bingo Party would start.

We used to go and pick up high school kids in our neighborhood and distribute the Bingo fliers in different neighborhoods and the local areas where my father was going to host the Bingo.

The amount of time and effort that went into the whole process was massive, i.e., from finding the right location for the Bingo night to the other arrangements like the seating, arranging the cards, and coming up with the themes, rewards, and refreshments. All of this was on top of his regular job on the weekdays. That was another prime example of dedication and self-discipline in my life which I saw.

I always thought he did not have to do it because nobody made him do all the work. It was not a chore or a duty, so why was he putting so much effort and time into this thing? Later, I realized what it all meant. He wanted to be more productive. Of course, the financial element of the whole thing was a factor behind all that, but I felt it was his way of being liberated from the mundane life and the rut he was during his weekdays. My dad often repeated to me, "Stay off the Plantation."

The term "Plantation" here means the idea of doing a "job." He had been doing one, as did my mother, so why would he say this to me? Later in life, I realized the importance of this phrase when I did my first job.

Technically, it was not a real job because I worked as a summer Louisiana legislature page when they were in session. It always started in the 2nd quarter of every year and ended during the first week in June. During that time, I got the experience of working for someone else, and it was then I realized what my father actually meant.

Dedicating all your energy, time and effort to someone else's dream or cause doesn't provide the satisfaction one gets when working for himself. Practically thinking, it is not fulfilling in terms of rewards, either. The one doing the hard yards always gets paid less, and the one with the dream and the risk always makes it big.

Besides all these qualities instilled in me, another quality I acquired over time was how to be a people person. I have always been an extrovert person and don't shy away from any situations; I know I would face them confidently. I would describe my feelings, opinions, and views very openly. It had a lot to do with the environment of my household, which provided me with this freedom. Over time, I cultivated this personality trait of mine into a very effective skill that helped me in many ways. Thus, it became a significant factor in my business life and made me successful. For this trait, among other things, I owe it to my father.

I grew up in a political household, and my dad was involved in local politics. He had the knack and expertise to fight for the little guy or the underdog. Like many of us, it was his natural instinct to support these guys to level the playing field against the mighty Goliaths.

He was very active in all the years he was involved. I was not involved in politics, nor have I been to date. One of the primary reasons is that during my father's political years, I saw the ugly side of politics. I've peeked behind the curtain and have discovered how dirty it can get. Politics is war without guns; it was a business I was not getting into. It wasn't for me, but I was always observant of him all these years. I would notice his mannerisms and habits in front of many people, how he reacted with his constituents, and the strategies and skills he showed in solving the problems of his people.

Following him during all these events and times, I cultivated the skill of being a people person, which has benefited me in business to this day.

***

Despite growing up around all the entrepreneurs, I did not want to become a businessman or an entrepreneur at first; in fact, I wanted to be a priest. My earliest memory of wanting to be a priest was when I was 10 or 12 years old. The idea of becoming one developed when I was an altar boy in our local Catholic church. During that time, I looked up to our priest. I might not remember the exact reason, but his charisma and personality showcased self-confidence and poise.

If you observe, these qualities are common in many businesspersons and entrepreneurs. Besides, religion and faith were vital parts of the community and the place where I grew up. The role and reputation of a priest, especially in those times, were nothing short of a celebrity. They were a big deal.

Despite considering to become a priest seriously, I took no action. I was pulled in a different direction when I reached my puberty years. Again, all these small, random events and things went in a specific direction and order and, in the end, worked for me. If I had become a priest, my life trajectory would have been different and perhaps the opposite. Another major, or you can say the practical reason was that priests could not marry. So, I decided that life was not meant for me.

Although I did not become a priest, the role of faith and religion have played a significant part in my life in numerous ways, directly and indirectly, which are indescribable. I was and am always attracted to the Creator. Again, this is the unexplainable category, but I felt a connection with the Creator. Spirituality has been an essential part of my life. I loved to pray, and I used to look at the sky. As I did this, I always felt connected, as if someone was looking back at me.

\*\*\*

My idea of becoming an entrepreneur unknowingly came to me when I pretended to be a banker while playing. My brothers, sister, and I used to play many role-playing games. The idea of me becoming a banker in one of the games came out of my imagination as I wanted to look and feel successful.

Of course, in the beginning, I did not actively follow the path of becoming a businessman. I graduated from Jeanerette Senior High, went to Grambling University for one semester, and then transferred to Southern University in Baton Rouge, Louisiana. With so many entrepreneurial role models in my life while growing up, it was inevitable for me not to follow that path.

Still, the gift of entrepreneurship came from the Creator in one way or another. He provided me with so many entrepreneurs in my life and then let me learn from them so I could experience everything firsthand.

The event that pushed me into entrepreneurship came when I was going into my senior year in college. My life took an unexpected turn out of nowhere. I got a call from my older brother about our old man not paying my bills anymore and I had to make it on my own.

"Hey man, your old man is not going to pay your bills anymore. So, you will have to go find some work or something," my brother told me.

I felt like my whole world suddenly got upside down. I had so many questions running through my mind that I couldn't say anything. After he told me, I just fell down on my knees and started crying, tears dropping, my body shaking, and I didn't know what to do except pray. My hands joined together, and I looked up toward the sky and started praying.

I prayed and cried the whole night. It still is one of the most challenging nights of my life. The night passed, and the sun came up. It was a clear morning, and so was my mind. I felt comfort and clarity. All those years of learning from my family's dedication and self-discipline clicked in me, and I was ready to take on the world.

I developed a plan of some sort in my mind on how to tackle this tragedy, but I still had not figured out many pieces. So during that weekend, a family meeting was called. The reason behind this tragedy in my life was the state. It was not just my tragedy; my dad and family also felt the pain as the state had decided not to fund my dad's business and pushed him out of business.

Again, all these small or random things were connected back then as I looked through them. If one thing or event had gone either way out of all these things, the story would have been different. I said earlier that the gift of entrepreneurship came from the Creator because, after all the fiasco, my oldest brother told me to take over the new venture in substance abuse counseling.

I jumped on it and did it. I put a lot of effort, energy, and time into that business. I applied what I had learned throughout my early days in that business. I was persistent, committed, and dedicated in that business every day. All of these things resulted in me making that company a million dollar worth just when I was only 21 years old.

I felt and knew deep down that my family did not think of me much at that time. It was not like they were not supportive or did not help me, but I felt they knew that the business would not last much longer. Or perhaps I would lose it all and be dependent on them again.

Despite all odds, I proved everyone wrong, including myself, because it was not till then I realized my potential and abilities. From the ashes of a tragedy, I rose. It was from this point that my love story with entrepreneurship started. From then on, I went on to do many more things in different businesses.

# Chapter 2

In 2007, I had just come out of a very dark phase in my life. I had spent seven years in what I call the 'Desert of Despair'. At that time, I was living with my girlfriend in Houston, Texas, trying to rebuild my life.

Then, the unexpected happened. A phone call from my brother, Omar, turned out to be the catalyst that would change circumstances. Omar had been working in the elderly care business and had an idea for starting a business in the field. He asked me to partner with him and take on this challenge.

It was an opportunity I couldn't refuse. I thought, "What do I have to lose at this point?" After all, I had been without money for a long time. The call from my brother was a blessing in disguise because it changed my life going forward.

With little to no capital, we both set out to build this new business. It was a daunting task, but we were determined to succeed. I was willing to take on any challenge and work hard to make the business successful.

There were many hurdles to overcome on this journey, but my brother and I never lost our vision. We worked tirelessly, and our efforts paid off slowly but surely.

The man who had once been lost in the darkness had found a new purpose in life. I was now helping people in their old age, providing them with care, and making a difference in their lives. I was grateful to my creator for giving me this opportunity. It was a reminder from the creator that no matter how dark the present may look, there will always be light for a better tomorrow.

Before jumping into the specifics of my journey in the elderly business with my brother, let me give you a brief background of the elderly care business in America.

The elderly care business in America has a long and evolving history shaped by various factors such as social changes, economic conditions, and government policies.

In the early 20th century, elderly care was primarily provided by family members or in institutional settings such as almshouses or poorhouses. However, as more elderly people moved to urban areas, the demand for professional elderly care services increased. This led to the emergence of private nursing homes and retirement communities, which were typically run by religious organizations or philanthropists.

During the 1930-60s, the second world war and the Great Depression brought significant changes to elderly care in America. The first federal program for the elderly came into being in 1935. It provided financial assistance to retired workers.

In the 1950s and 1960s, Medicare and Medicaid were created to provide healthcare coverage for the elderly and low-income individuals. The introduction of these programs sparked a rapid expansion of the elderly care industry, with many private companies entering the market.

The 1970s-1990s. The 1970s and 1980s saw a shift towards a more market-oriented approach to elderly care, with the growth of for-profit nursing homes and assisted living facilities. These businesses focused on providing high-quality services to attract customers and expand their market share. The 1990s saw further growth in the industry, with the rise of home healthcare services and hospice care.

We started with little to nothing. Starting an elderly care business is difficult, especially with little to no capital. But we were determined to make it work.

Omar paid for the office rent and license fee, while we used some old furniture we had lying around for our small office. We didn't need a huge office to operate, so we kept things simple. The state didn't require us to have a large space, which made things a little easier.

However, the company still had to pay my brother back the money he had invested in the business. It was a small amount, but it felt like a million dollars. I had to make it work and make my second million-dollar business happen.

After this, more initial hurdles started to arrive. Getting a license to operate our business was the first hurdle we had to overcome. It wasn't an easy process and took a lot of time and effort. Once we got the license, we had to start marketing our business and finding clients.

The first step in providing care for the elderly is identifying those who need it. This can be done in several ways, but one effective strategy is to work with individuals who already have knowledge of the elderly in the community.

In this case, Miss Janie was the key to identifying those who needed care. She had an extensive network and knowledge of the elderly population in the community. Working with her, we identified those who required our services and developed a list of potential clients. It was a slow and challenging process.

At first, the business was struggling to get off the ground. It wasn't until August 2007 that we got our first Medicaid cheque. The first Medicaid check I got was a life-changing moment for me. After a long and arduous process, I finally received the check for $9K. The relief I felt was overwhelming, and I knew my bills would get paid.

We also had to wait 30 days for the state to send us a care plan for our clients. It was a long and frustrating process, and it affected our revenue. We had to learn to be patient and persistent, even when things weren't going our way.

In today's world, social media and online advertising dominate the marketing landscape. However, word of mouth was the most powerful tool for getting new clients. We were able to leverage our existing clients to spread the word about our business. Because we had developed trust with our clients which lead to referrals.

The art of personal touch helped us set apart from others in the same industry. We went above and beyond for our clients by showing up to their homes and ensuring they feel cared for.

As word of mouth spread, our business started to grow. Another significant challenge was finding well-certified nursing assistants. The good ones were hard to find, and we spent time and effort searching for the right people to join our team. We had to ensure that our employees were compassionate, caring, and dedicated to their work.

Despite the initial challenges, we were determined to make our business work. We worked hard and passionately to build our reputation in the community and provided excellent care to our clients. We treated our employees like family and created a positive work environment.

Much of the credit for the initial grind and hustle goes to Miss Janie. I met her at one of the Christmas parties for the first time. The annual company Christmas party was always a big event. It was a chance for employees to socialize outside of the office and for management to show appreciation for employees' efforts throughout the year. We exchanged pleasantries, and I immediately sensed that she was serious about her work.

Over the next few months, I had several opportunities to work with Miss Janie. She was always professional and efficient, but she also had a warmth and kindness that made it easy to work with her. We often had long conversations about the business and our shared goals, and I found that I really enjoyed her company.

One thing that impressed me about Miss Janie was her dedication to her work. She was always on top of things and never let anything slip through the cracks. I knew I could count on her to make it happen if I needed something done. I admired her intelligence, her professionalism, and her dedication to her work.

To overcome more challenges in our business, we developed a new strategy that involved utilizing family members to provide care. We encouraged certified nursing assistants who had family members in need of care to take on the role of caregiver. This approach was a win-win for both the family member and the client. The family member was able to provide care for their loved one while also earning an income. At the same time, the client received quality care from someone they already knew and trusted.

At first, when the business started gathering pace, I was relieved for a bit. While all this was happening, I thought I could finally pay my bills on time. I had been struggling to make ends meet for so long that I gave up hope of ever becoming a millionaire. But eventually, I became a certified millionaire from this business.

But my dreams didn't stop there. I wanted to expand the practice and serve other cities and communities. I spent countless hours brainstorming and researching the best ways to maximize the region and make the most money possible.

I knew opening other offices and would be the best way to achieve this goal. I pitched the idea to Omar and he loved it. So, we began the process of expanding the business.

It wasn't an easy journey. I spent at least 55 hours a week and weekends brainstorming on opening other locations and other businesses.

Over time, our business grew, and we hired more employees and opened a second office.

We were excited to bring our services to new customers who needed our help. We understood that expanding the business would require additional investments, but we were confident in our plan and budgeted accordingly.

Our strategy was to establish our business in one city, perfect our services and build a strong customer base before expanding to other cities. We wanted to ensure that our reputation and quality of service were maintained throughout our expansion.

We were successful in doing so and were able to establish our business in a new location.

The 1/3 theory in business was a crucial aspect of our expansion. We followed this theory, which helped us maintain a healthy financial structure that allowed us to continue growing.

The 1/3 theory in business is a popular financial strategy that can be used to ensure a company's growth and success. This theory recommends that a company allocates one-third of its profits to reinvest in the business, one-third be saved, and one-third be distributed as profits to the owners. Following this strategy allows a company to maintain a healthy financial structure, reduce risk, and continue to expand.

Reinvesting one-third of the profits into the business is a smart strategy to keep up with changing industry trends and consumer demands. A company can use the funds to upgrade equipment, expand its product line, hire more employees, or even open a new location. A company can stay competitive and relevant in the market by reinvesting in the business.

Saving one-third of the profits can be beneficial in times of economic uncertainty or downturn. A financial cushion can help a company weather unexpected expenses, such as repairs or emergencies. It can also allow the company to save for future growth, such as expanding into new markets or acquiring other businesses.

Distributing one-third of the profits as profits to the owners can provide financial rewards and incentives for their hard work and investment. The owners can use the funds for personal expenses or other ventures. It is important to note that this third should not be distributed until the other two-thirds have been allocated appropriately. Otherwise, it may negatively impact the company's financial structure and hinder future growth.

For example, a small retail business with a net profit of $100,000 might follow the 1/3 theory in the following way:

Reinvesting one-third ($33,333) of their profits into the business by expanding their product line and renovating their store to attract more customers.

Saving one-third ($33,333) of their profits to use as a financial cushion or to invest in future growth opportunities.

Distributing one-third ($33,333) of their profits as profits to the business owner(s) as a reward for their hard work and investment in the company.

Following the 1/3 theory, the business can maintain a healthy financial structure to grow and expand. It also helps to reduce risk and provides financial rewards for the business owner(s).

The next crucial step in our expansion was applying for a new business license. The process of applying for the license was simple, but ensuring that all the necessary information and documents were in order was important. Once we submitted our application, we waited for the inspectors to come and evaluate our business. It was nerve-wracking to wait for the results, but we were confident in our abilities and knew we had followed all the rules and regulations.

In the end, our hard work and perseverance paid off. We received our license to operate in the new city and brought our services to more people in need. We were thrilled to see our business grow and expand beyond our initial expectations.

In my first business venture after three years, I was burnt out. I was a wreck emotionally, physically, and spiritually. I had been so focused on achieving my dreams that I had neglected my well-being. But this time I was up for the challenge.

It was time for me to step back and reflect on what was important. I realized that my ambition had taken over my life, and I had forgotten to enjoy the journey. I had been so focused on achieving the goals I missed out on life's simple pleasures.

I made a conscious effort to slow down and take care of myself. I also learned to delegate tasks and trust others to help me achieve my goals.

After taking some time off to reflect and recharge, I returned to the business with a new perspective. But more importantly, I had found a sense of fulfillment that I had been missing. I was no longer just chasing after money and success; I was making a difference in people's lives. I had found a balance between achieving my dreams and enjoying the journey.

Besides the money, one of the major reasons for making the business successful was my empathy toward my clients. In today's competitive business world, it can be easy to get caught up in pursuing profits and overlook the importance of empathy. However, the truth is that empathy can be a powerful tool in building a successful business.

Many businesses focus solely on making a profit, but empathy is equally important. When you care about your clients and their needs, you can build long-lasting relationships that benefit both you and them.

The first step to building empathy in business is listening to your clients. When you take the time to understand their needs and concerns, you can tailor your services to meet their specific needs.

In my case, understanding the needs of clients with chronic diseases was essential. I took time to sit with them and listen to them. This exercise not only helped the clients feel heard but also helped my business grow.

The interactions between clients and business owners can make or break a business. Positive interactions can lead to repeat business and referrals. Honesty and communication are crucial in any business relationship. At the same time, a lack of communication can destroy a business. This strategy can do wonders, especially for a business with huge competition.

Becoming a millionaire was a dream come true, but it was not without its challenges. I learned that caring for oneself and balancing between ambition and fulfillment is important. Anything is possible with hard work, perseverance, and a little reflection.

Faith again played a crucial part during all these phases of my life. I was very spiritual and humble during this period. The reason is a life-altering experience that happened to me in April 2008.

In life, certain events change us in ways we never imagined possible. For some, it could be a major milestone or a life-altering event. For others, it could be a spiritual experience that transforms their entire being.

The incident occurred during a Catholic service when I suddenly had an out-of-body experience. The experience is indescribable in words, but you can imagine it as a feeling of love.

I felt the love of my creator, which humbled me. This love was so intense that you could compare it to the purest form of love, which comes from a mother in this world. And then multiply it seven times.

The experience of my soul jumping out of my body lasted only three seconds in real time, but it felt like a long time. It was so intense that I might not want to return from that experience if I could experience it again.

This experience of feeling my creator's love was life-changing. From that moment on, my connection with faith and spirituality became more powerful.

Spiritual experiences are known to be transformative. They often lead to a deeper understanding of the self, the universe, and their interconnectedness. In this case, I, too, connected with something greater than myself, giving me a deeper appreciation of life.

This experience transformed the individual's entire being, and they began seeing the world differently. Their connection with faith and spirituality became essential to their whole life journey.

This incident allowed me to see beyond the physical realm and experience a sense of oneness with everything. This experience serves as a reminder that there is more to life than what meets the eye and that sometimes, the most profound experiences can happen in the most unexpected ways.

# Chapter 3

My elderly care business was going successful and profitable. My brother and I were achieving new heights in the business. All our hard work and business acumen were bearing fruits. But one day, we faced a major hurdle in our journey.

It was a typical weekday morning, and the staff was preparing for the day to offer great services to our elderly clients. Suddenly, the police burst down our door with guns blazing. Police cars were all over our office. The scene was like a movie in which police crackdown the warehouse of a major drug lord or someone selling crack or meth. Everyone was shocked and taken aback.

It was a surreal experience, and I could not believe this was happening. I thought to myself, "why would anyone do this type of thing when we did everything right?"

At first, I had a lot of questions. My mind was filled with confusion and scenarios. Later on, the reason was revealed. Apparently, the state monitor did not like how Omar and our company's attorney spoke to her in one of the interactions.

She had come out to monitor us. All of our books were in order. Despite her best efforts, she could not find anything to get us in trouble or shut down. So, it was her ego that got our office raided. It still fathoms me how another person's ego and bad intentions can ruin our efforts and hard work. We built everything from scratch, and another person's envy took it all over in a flash.

The raid was a traumatic experience for us, and we were devastated by the loss of our computers and records. The police seized everything in our office, leaving us with nothing to continue running our business. Our business took a hit initially, and we had no idea what to do next. We knew we had done nothing wrong but were treated like criminals.

After the raid, we were served papers claiming all kinds of things against our office manager and staff. It was a list of false accusations. We were good bookkeepers and went by the letter of the law. We were determined to fight back because we didn't do anything wrong. The truth was on our side.

Growing up, my late dad told us to always prepare for war or fight. This doesn't necessarily mean in literal terms but to be ready to stand your ground and retaliate.

So my brother and I regrouped and got our team of Attorneys ready to answer all the accusations. After the initial confusion and worry, we were confident of striking back.

At the time, word got out in the community that we got raided. There were murmurs among our clients and community. But not for long because our business professionalism overcame that obstacle. People knew us. Our clients knew us and what we were about.

Our intentions and aim were to help the elderly and not commit crimes, which they were trying to portray. And they failed and failed miserably. It did not affect the business at all, and we kept moving along. We maintained a positive attitude and continued to provide quality care for our elderly clients.

The raid on our office or other accusations did not have a bad mental impact on me. When we opened up the business, I had an idea that this was an obstacle we had to face. But I never thought it would get to this level.

Although I did not let all of these things affect me, I had thought about getting out of the elderly care business even before that. After these events, I had a lot of sleepless nights. The thoughts of what I would do next after this business or how will I sustain my life wandered through my mind. I felt burnt out and thought this was no way I could run a business under all these circumstances.

Despite all the determination, the stress and strain of the situation were immense. It took a toll on our personal lives as well. We had to constantly deal with the fallout from the raid, and it was a difficult time.

But whenever we felt down, the fire to fight back burnt again, and we constantly pursued to clear our names.

It was a long and grueling process, but we knew we had to do it. We could not let our hard work go to waste. We fought back with everything we had. We knew that the state monitor had no proof to back them up. We provided all the relevant documentation and evidence proving we complied with all regulations.

Eventually, In 2014 my brother received a phone call, and all charges were dropped. The lawyers handled everything after our submission of all the relevant documents.

It was a huge relief for both Omar and me. We had been through a difficult time but came out stronger on the other side. It was a reminder that you have to be prepared for anything in business. It is not always smooth sailing, and there will be obstacles along the way.

From 2014 to 2016, I was still attached to the elderly care business. Despite the setbacks, my brother and I turned it into a million-dollar business. The process of building our million-dollar business was using the same techniques I had used when I first got into the elderly care business.

I used professionalism, courtesy, and compassion. And then relied on word of mouth because our services were top-notch. Using those three principles got us into a great service provider. One cannot deny that we were a great benefit to our community.

In terms of financing, the business we used was medical factoring. Medical factoring is when you leverage your billing to get 80% upfront for your billing and 20% in escrow.

It is a financial strategy that is often used by healthcare providers to obtain quick cash flow for their business. It involves selling your accounts receivable to a third-party company, known as a factor, in exchange for a lump sum of cash.

One of the advantages of this strategy is that a third party is responsible for collecting payments from insurance companies or patients themselves. So, we service providers have more time on our hands, which we can divert into providing more quality care.

One of the main advantages of medical factoring is that it provides a predictable source of financing and does not require any credit check or collateral. So basically, it improves your cash flow, and you avoid the risk of late or unpaid bills.

Medical factoring is a popular financing strategy for healthcare providers who need quick cash flow and want to reduce their administrative burden. Whether you are a small practice or a large hospital, medical factoring can provide the resources needed to grow your business and provide quality patient care.1

If I look back, the raid on our office taught me some valuable lessons.

First and foremost, it reminded me of the importance of good business practices. We always ensured that our books were in order and complied with all regulations. It was this commitment to professionalism that ultimately saved us.

Secondly, it reminded me of the importance of being prepared for anything. Even when you think everything is going smoothly in the business, you must be prepared to tackle unexpected hurdles. But if you stay true to your values and yourself, you can overcome anything.

Lastly, it reminded me of the importance of perseverance. It would have been easy to give up and walk away from the business after the raid. But we did not do that. We fought back with everything we had and came out stronger on the other side.

Eventually, I was burnt out from the elderly care business and decided to switch to the medicinal Cannabis industry. That transition is an interesting story I will tell in the next chapter. Although I always felt sympathy for my clients because many relied on our services, we were indeed making a change in their lives. But that sympathy and feelings for my clients were overpowered by the exhaustion caused by this business.

---

[1] Medical Factoring - Factoring | Green Capital Funding, LLC (greencapfunding.com)

It is necessary to recognize that point where you have to make decisions like this in business because it is not always about money.

Money is the byproduct of your excellence, and you will not excel if your heart and mind are not into it. If a certain business is taking a toll on you despite it being successful, you have to prioritize your health every time.

# Chapter 4

In 2016, after a decade of working in the elderly care business, I made the difficult decision to leave the industry for good. However, I had a great time in the business despite its challenges. I, along with my brother, made it successful.

We felt we had made a difference in the community with our services. The clients loved us, and we loved and cared for them. I remember the early days were challenging. I worked long hours, often sacrificing time with family and friends, to get the business up and running. But seeing the positive impact that our services had on our clients made it all worthwhile. It was not a healthy lifestyle. So, I decided to leave it.

There comes the point where you have to decide when to leave a business, that "when" is important.

Firstly, it is vital to understand that quitting or leaving a successful business is not a sign of failure. Sometimes, businessmen or entrepreneurs may feel like they have to continue running their businesses, even if they are not enjoying it. The only reason being the money and an established stream of income. However, continuing to run a business that no longer aligns with your future goals can lead to burnout.

Additionally, unhappiness and unfulfillment can creep on you as they did creep up on me. The entrepreneur must have a heart in his venture. The person would be excited to go to work, and it should fulfill his desires other than money. But, like me, it can become overwhelming if you have to deal with legal and regulatory issues and encounter industry disruption with all the work that the business demands.

However, one should analyze and assess their personal and professional goals before leaving a successful business. One should take the plunge if the new business or venture aligns with those interests and goals. Or, one can manage multiple businesses as well if they hire responsible people.

In many businesses, the mastermind behind the scenes delegates all the work, just like I did with the cannabis industry. We will go into that in detail in the later chapters, but at that time, I felt I could not delegate the elderly care business, so I decided to leave it and move on.

## Transitioning to the Mental Health Business

Initially, I had no clear plan or idea of what to do next. But I knew I was ready for a change. Before going into the details about what came next, we first had to decide what to do with this business. Whom to give it to? Who will be as compassionate toward the clients as we were? These were the questions that were standing in front of me. After giving it much thought, the only people who came to mind were my family.

I handed over the entire business to my family members. The process of transitioning out of my brother from the elderly care business had started, but it presented its own set of challenges too. We were exhausted from the elderly care business, sure! But we did not want to go back to being broke or blow up our savings because we did not have a new idea or a plan.

Never mind, we went ahead with it. I sold my elderly care business to my mom. She was happy with it and took great care of it. She eventually sold it in 2017.

The other elderly business I gave to my sister, which she still operates to this day. It was important that the clients and staff should be happy with these changes and that the flow of the business's profit didn't break. We were successful in transitioning these changes smoothly. Ultimately, everyone was satisfied, including the clients and the staff.

For us, the next idea, or you can say the challenge was to enter into the outpatient mental health business. We were excited about the potential to make a difference in this business as well but in a different way.

We put in the initial grind and hustle in this business also. We worked for long hours and put in more effort than before. But it did not turn out to be what we were hoping for. The business had its own set of challenges and setbacks, and we realized that it was not worth our while to put more time, effort, and money into this. So, we decided to leave it.

Just like it is important to realize and assess when to leave a successful business, it is also important to realize when to get out when the ship starts to sink. Our decision to leave the elderly business was good and well thought out. But our decision to enter into the outpatient mental health business was not.

That's how it is, especially in the game of entrepreneurship. One day you think you have cracked it, and the next day life happens. It is important to analyze and assess the scope of the venture you are getting into. Which we eventually did with the cannabis industry. We learned our lesson from here.

## Brief History of Criminalization of Cannabis

One day a gold mind kind of opportunity presented itself to us. I still think that it had something to do with my faith in the Creator and his rewarding me.

In 2016, my brother received a phone call from a friend named Harold. He told us that the state would soon be awarding dispensary licenses to companies looking to enter the cannabis industry. It was a big deal and a golden opportunity. I was intrigued and excited beyond my wildest imagination. But I was hesitant too.

To understand why it was such a big deal and why I was initially hesitant, I need to provide you with some context. To do this, let me provide you with some hardcore history and facts about this whole situation of medicinal cannabis legalization.

First, it is important to keep in mind and understand that the issue of cannabis legalization is not exclusive or unique to the state of Louisiana. It is a major national issue that has been hovering in the air for decades.

In the United States of America, cannabis was first criminalized in the 1930s. At that time, there were concerns and perceptions that this plant would supposedly have a negative effect on society. Obviously, at that time, people were not aware of its medicinal qualities.

This is why the criminalization of cannabis in the United States of America can be traced back to the early 20th century. In 1937, the Marijuana Tax came into existence. The federal government passed it. This rule effectively banned the use, sale, and cultivation of cannabis. Prior to this, cannabis was not widely seen as a harmful substance and was even used medicinally in some cases.

It is important to note that the criminalization of cannabis had racial and political motivations. The use of cannabis was associated with Mexican immigrants and black jazz musicians. Many politicians used anti-immigrant and anti-black sentiment to push for its prohibition.

Additionally, the head of the Federal Bureau of Narcotics, Harry Anslinger, led a campaign to demonize cannabis by spreading false information about its effects, such as claiming that it caused insanity and violence.

President Richard M. Nixon also played a crucial negative role in this entire fiasco. He criminalized all forms of drugs, including cannabis. And he did it deliberately because it was legal, just like everything else before that. He started a war on drugs.

He especially did it to hurt the Black and Brown communities. What is appalling and sad is that these policies continued under future administrations after him. The racial disparities in cannabis-related arrests and convictions have been well-documented.

Black people were being arrested nearly four times more than white people for cannabis-related offenses. However, the usage rates are very similar among both of them. Because of this, a number of people were incarcerated for non-violent drug offenses.2

It tore apart families and ruined lives. To this day, it is still not fully legalized in the U.S.A. These events had a major impact on everyone, particularly on the Black and Brown communities. It caused so much damage to us for decades and generations.

## Cannabis Legalization in Louisiana

Despite the harms caused by criminalization, Louisiana technically legalized cannabis for medical purposes in 1978 and 1991. In 1978 Governor Edwin Edwards signed a law that created the Marijuana Prescription Review board. The board's purpose was to give the Health and Human Resources responsibility to provide contracts to national groups for the product and distribution.

Then in 1991, the Legislature amended the 1978 law and, this time, they added spastic quadriplegia to the list of ailments that can be qualified for the that qualify for medical marijuana. The state never set up ways and means to distribute it but guess what? The distribution methods were never established, so it didn't help anyone.

However, even as more states began to legalize cannabis, it remained illegal at the federal level. This created a complicated legal landscape for cannabis businesses, as they had to navigate both state and federal laws.

---

[2] War on Drugs - Timeline in America, Definition & Facts - HISTORY

In 2013, the Obama administration issued a memo that stated it would not interfere with state cannabis laws as long as certain criteria were met, but this policy was not codified into law.3

Eventually, in 2015, when a Medical Marijuana bill was introduced and signed into law by Governor Bobby Jindal, Louisiana finally had a system in place. A system for the growth, distribution, and prescription of medicinal cannabis. This has provided many people with the medical help they need and deserve.

Overall, the history of cannabis legalization in Louisiana is a complex and ongoing story that is intertwined with issues of social justice and racial inequality. I won't go into much detail because the atrocities and the events are so much more that this book will not be enough.

But coming back to the event of us getting the opportunity to enter the cannabis industry.

## Getting into the Cannabis Industry

Despite all the initial hesitations, as a business opportunity, realizing that there was a chance to enter into the cannabis industry was huge. After our outpatient mental business, this seemed like a perfect opportunity to take a leap. It was not like Harold wanted us to be in this business, but the other way around. After the initial call, we were chasing him about the details and required information.

---

[3] Nuance Communications, Inc. (justice.gov)

Because this time, I wanted to be prepared for the next business. I wanted to analyze every aspect before entering the medical cannabis industry.

Initially, we told only our Dad about this opportunity, and that is because he could have helped us by bringing a pharmacist. This did not happen, and when we did get the pharmacist, we were scammed, but that's the story for another chapter.

Entering the cannabis industry was a lucrative opportunity for my brother and me. With the legalization of medical marijuana in Louisiana, I saw the market with high demand and low competition. The competition was low because getting the license was itself a herculean task. But even with that in mind, I thought the industry was a "gold mine."

Starting a venture in the cannabis industry requires major investment and carries high risk. The cost of obtaining a dispensary license alone can range from $10,000 to $50,000, depending on the state. There are also costs associated with securing a location, hiring staff, purchasing equipment, and obtaining inventory.

In addition, the cannabis industry is subject to stringent regulations that can be difficult to navigate. No doubt it had high profits, but due to its strict regulations, there were bound to be more challenges that were visible on the surface.

I knew that the regulatory landscape around cannabis was constantly changing. As we discussed in its brief history, it is visible that different laws and regulations were being applied, which varied from state to state. This was something that did create uncertainty in my mind and plans for the future.

However, despite creating thorough research or analysis, I went with my business instinct and gut. It was this instinct, with the mix of strategies that I learned, that had gotten me to this point. I knew I had to put more work and effort into this, even in the initial stage, than the businesses before.

Building the team and finding the right people to hire was like Mount Everest, which I had to climb. But I took the risk. Believe it or not, I was somehow confident despite having so many challenges. Maybe it was my Creator's power backing me up or my skills, but it got me through.

Even if we look at it from a business point of view, it makes sense. Because it was a promising market with potential, I saw that it would bring much-needed relief to patients suffering from a variety of medical conditions. I also saw the opportunity of introducing other products in this business too way before. Overall, I contemplated all these factors before entering the industry.

Here is an important lesson for entrepreneurs in this chapter from my example. The importance of thorough research and analysis before entering any new business venture. In addition to the strong connections in the relevant industry.

The first and critical step in analyzing a business opportunity is relevant to research. This involves gathering information about the industry. What is the market size? Who are the competitors, and how do they operate? What are they lacking? What will be your USP? Who are the target customers? You should have the answer to all of these questions before entering into the relevant business.

Conducting market research is essential to determine whether there is a demand for the product or service and whether there is potential for growth in the industry.

Once you have done your research, the next step is to assess the potential profitability of the business. This involves analyzing the financials of the business from start to end. What will be the revenue, and from which area will you get more of it? What will be the expenses? What will be the profit margins? Although it is hard to accurately predict and assess all of these things, one can come close.

Even after having the answers to all these questions, something else related to these can surprise you. But at least you will be better prepared. It is important to consider the business's short-term and long-term financial outlook because then you can spot a problem from a mile and solve it.

Another important factor to consider is the management team behind the business. A strong management team can make all the difference in the success of a business. It's important to assess the management team's skills, experience, and track record to ensure they have the expertise and leadership necessary to drive the business forward.

All of these things are absolutely important before investing or starting a new business. Without factoring all these in, there is a high chance that you will lose a lot of money. These factors are like the airbags in a car. You hope that you don't need them, but it is necessary to have them. Besides, if there is a discrepancy or problem in the business you are delving into, there is a good chance you will find it during all this research.

Even after all this research and assessment, if you have a strong gut feeling about a business or a venture, don't hesitate to take action. The power of conviction and taking the right action at the right time often overpowers all this assessment. But one should be confident and business savvy in their action and conviction.

Usually, that confidence and acumen come from experiences and self-learning. There is no alternative to experience, but if you are unable to experience something, self-learning is the way to go. This book is just a drop in the ocean of knowledge about the techniques and principles of entrepreneurship.

But I am hoping it will provide a unique perspective to you about all the entrepreneur techniques, strategies, and principles used today by paralleling my journey in multiple businesses.

Although after assessing many factors, what prompted me toward the cannabis industry was my gut. I want to mention that in the case of the cannabis industry, it was particularly important for me to be aware of the legal and regulatory environment.

Similarly, there are many businesses where these things also play their part. It is absolutely necessary to make yourself aware of all these regulations and the political climate in which your business is relevant. These things play a major role in the success of a business.

In conclusion, analyzing a business opportunity is an important step in the entrepreneurial process. By taking a systematic and analytical approach, entrepreneurs can identify opportunities with the greatest potential for success and avoid costly mistakes.

# Chapter 5

The legalization of medicinal cannabis was a turning point in the history of Louisiana, as I mentioned before. It opened up a new avenue for entrepreneurs looking for exciting opportunities. The demand of entering into medical cannabis was high. This is why the state government created a regulatory framework allowing licensed dispensaries to provide patients access to safe and effective cannabis products.

However, acquiring a license to operate a medicinal cannabis dispensary in Louisiana was herculean. Throughout the coming chapters, I will discuss the preparations and the procedures for acquiring this license and the lessons I learned as an entrepreneur. But even before that, there were other initial hurdles that my brother and I faced.

The first significant hurdle in the journey was finding a qualified pharmacist to join our team. The state required that each licensed dispensary have a licensed pharmacist on staff to oversee medication dispensing. Finding a pharmacist who had experience with cannabis was not an easy task. Cannabis is still considered a Schedule I drug by the federal government, which means that pharmacists are not trained in its use or administration.

It took us months to find the right person with the necessary experience and qualifications to meet the state's requirements. Our Dad played a vital role in this aspect as we found the pharmacist through his recommendation. She was a friend of my Dad's wife, and she had expressed an interest in working with us. At first, everything seemed good about her. She was perfect in a lot of sense. Still, we had several discussions with her, after which she agreed to our percentage and was ready to sign the agreement with our company.

However, after two weeks, we noticed something was not right. The pharmacist had stopped returning our calls. We have not received any updates from her. We were worried, and it was then that we received a call from one of our good friends who told us that the pharmacist had approached him. Her plan was exposed as she wanted to cut us out of the deal.

We were shocked and disappointed by her actions. It was disheartening to see someone we had trusted turn against us and try to take advantage of our hard work. By this act of hers, you can understand how much of a lucrative opportunity the medicinal cannabis business was. Everyone wanted a shot at it. What hurt us more at that point was the time and effort we had already put into finding the right pharmacist. Now we were facing two setbacks. The situation with the current pharmacist and finding a new one. Her betrayal had derailed our plans, which was frustrating.

However, we did not let these setbacks discourage us. We knew challenges would be along the way and were prepared to face them head-on. Our plan of action was to cut ties with the pharmacist at first. Then we continued searching for a qualified pharmacist committed to working with us.

We searched long and wide in our area but couldn't find one at first. The whole task had become more frustrating. At that time, I thought we would have to find the pharmacist by any means necessary because we had too much to lose. I was even willing to advertise on the Internet for a good one. Eventually, we started calling everyone we knew, and after a tiresome search for months, we found one. He was an ideal candidate too. He had 30 years of experience of owning his own pharmacy. Additionally, he had a great track record with the community and the state board.

In retrospect, this incident taught us a valuable lesson. As entrepreneurs, we must be cautious and careful when dealing with people. We learned that having a clear agreement and working with people who share our values and commitment to success is essential.

Let this be a lesson to all fellow entrepreneurs, "A bird in the hand is better than two in the bush." Although our Dad had recommended the first pharmacist who tricked us, that did not hamper our relationship with him. Often these things are not in control of anybody, but it's important to keep the healthy relationships you already have intact.

As we embarked on the journey of acquiring a license for a medicinal cannabis dispensary in Louisiana, we knew that having a solid team was crucial to our success. While finding a qualified pharmacist was a significant challenge, assembling a team of dedicated and experienced individuals was equally important.

After securing the right pharmacist, Omar's next priority was to find a skilled and dedicated staff to help us run our dispensary. Finding the right employees is crucial to the success of any business, as it was ours. Many times, businessmen or companies tend to compromise on this aspect. Your business will take of itself in many aspects if you hire the right people for the right job. If you look at the examples of successful entrepreneurs and their companies, one common thing in them is the people they hired. Because if you want to cross the barrier of an average entrepreneur, you must learn to delegate work.

The one thing we did differently was that we hired individuals who were qualified and shared our commitment to patient care and compliance. After this, We hired effective attorneys and accountants. You probably would know that they are crucial to any business's success. However, in our case, they had a much bigger role because the legal and regulatory landscape surrounding the medicinal cannabis industry was complex and constantly evolving. We needed experienced attorneys who understood the industry's intricacies and could help us navigate the legal requirements.

Similarly, hiring skilled accountants who could manage our finances and ensure compliance with tax laws was essential. We were fortunate to have found excellent attorneys and accountants dedicated to our success and helped us navigate the industry's complexities.

Building a strong team was vital to our success in acquiring a license for a medicinal cannabis dispensary in Louisiana. We needed a qualified pharmacist, a skilled staff, and experienced attorneys and accountants to help us navigate the complex regulatory landscape. First and foremost, we recognized the importance of having a cohesive and capable team to make informed decisions and work effectively together. With our team in place, we gained the confidence to tackle the rigorous rules and regulations set forth by the state of Louisiana for acquiring a license to operate a medicinal cannabis dispensary. Meeting the state's requirements was crucial, so we compiled a comprehensive application with a detailed business plan, financial projections, security plan, and operating procedures.

Once we secured a pharmacist to join our team and submitted our application, our next challenge was finding a location for the dispensary that met the state's strict zoning laws. We had to be mindful of sensitive locations like schools and churches, which was a time-consuming task for the perfect spot. However, we persevered and eventually found a location that met all the state's requirements.

Finding the right contractors was the final piece of the puzzle. We needed reputable professionals with a track record of finishing projects on time.

To find such contractors, we turned to our local architecture firm, which had been in business for many years and had a wealth of experience in the industry. The firm not only provided us with referrals for contractors but also helped us navigate the complex and often confusing process of obtaining the necessary city and parish permits.

When selecting contractors, we took great care to ensure we were hiring highly skilled individuals with a proven track record of success. We asked for their list of references and accomplishments and thoroughly checked their credentials to ensure they were the right fit for our project.

We understood that the success of our dispensary depended on the quality of the contractors we hired. We needed individuals who could work quickly and efficiently while maintaining the highest quality and professionalism standards.

Fortunately, the contractors referred to us by our architecture firm met all of our requirements and expectations. They were highly skilled, professional, and always finished projects on time. Their work was of the highest quality, and they took great care to ensure that all aspects of the project were completed to our satisfaction.

Until now, you must have put it together that starting a medicinal cannabis dispensary requires a significant investment in building costs and operations. We had to secure financing to cover the cost of constructing the dispensary and purchasing inventory. We also had to ensure we had enough capital to cover ongoing expenses such as salaries, rent, utilities, and inventory.

The final hurdle we faced was the competition for the license. The state had a limited number of licenses available. The journey for the license was going to be more intense going ahead. We had to prepare a presentation and present it in front of the board of pharmacy. But that is the story for another chapter.

Building the team, reviewing the reading materials, and building the documents were all part of the preparation before the presentation. We wanted to be well prepared and different from all the other competitors. My idea was to create that edge between us and others so we could be more noticeable. There was significant competition among applicants. We had to ensure that our application was thorough and professional and differentiated us from our competitors.

Omar, the experienced and skilled entrepreneur he is, took charge of this preparation process. He worked tirelessly to ensure that we had everything in the right order to present it to the board of pharmacy. He spent countless hours reviewing every detail of our application to ensure it was thorough.

There are some major lessons that you need to understand from this chapter. These can help every entrepreneur who is starting or even thinking about starting. Initially, you can have the perfect business plan, massive investment, and perfect location, but it still can fail. These things are necessary and fine, but the people make the business work.

Again, I am stressing the point that you have to hire the right people and smartly too. You need to find individuals who are skilled, experienced, and have a passion for what they do. Hiring the right people can help you achieve your goals faster and create a positive and productive work environment.

After this, you have to take the approach of delegating the work. As a new entrepreneur, you may need to do everything yourself. If you're managing multiple businesses and aiming to create different income streams, it's important to avoid micromanaging.

Delegation is key, but it's crucial to clearly understand your expectations with your employees.

When delegating work, it's essential to be clear about your expectations. Ensure your employees understand what you need them to do, and provide them with the necessary tools and resources to complete the task successfully. It's also important to provide feedback and support throughout the process. It's important to create a positive and productive work environment. This can be achieved by treating your employees with respect.

The next major point I want to stress is about dealing with setbacks, especially while starting a new business. No matter how well you plan, there will be setbacks and obstacles along the way. However, dealing with these setbacks will ultimately determine your business's success.

First and foremost, it's important to understand that setbacks are a natural part of the business world. No matter how successful you are, there will always be obstacles and challenges that you need to overcome. The key is to remain focused and not let setbacks discourage you. In fact, setbacks can be a valuable learning experience that can help you improve your business and ultimately make it stronger.

Imagine if I had let the whole scenario of the first pharmacist affect me deeply. I might not have recovered from it. It would have been understandable for sure, but I did not let it impact me more than it deserved. Sure! It was a rough time. The whole scenario wasted a lot of our precious time and effort, but how I dealt with it made me the man I am today!

One of the most important things you can do when facing a setback is to stay calm and keep a positive attitude. It's easy to get caught up in the stress and frustration of the situation, but this will only make things worse. Instead, take a step back and assess the situation objectively. Ask yourself what went wrong and what you can do differently in the future to prevent similar setbacks from occurring. You have to think critically and practically in these situations and scenarios. You cannot let your emotions or feelings get the better of you, especially in terms of business.

Another important step is to seek advice and support from others. This could be from a mentor, business coach, or even other entrepreneurs who have gone through similar experiences, just like this book. If the situation is similar or you get its main gist, you can apply it to your situation. Guidance and insight are valuable at the time of dealing with a setback.

In addition to seeking advice, it's important to be proactive in finding solutions. This means addressing the problem head-on and developing a plan to overcome it. This may require making tough decisions or even pivoting your business strategy, but remaining flexible and open to change is important.

Another thing that you need to focus on is to make the business presentable. After reading about our journey, I am sure you must have put together how much we spent in the initial phase of the business. But it is important and will always remain important. Investing the money in the right place and department is key. This means having a clear vision and strategy and focusing on your business's appearance and how it is presented to potential customers.

Branding is one of the first things to consider when building a presentable business. Your brand should be memorable, unique, and reflective of the values and personality of your business. This includes everything from the name and logo to the overall aesthetic of your website and physical storefront (if applicable). This is what we did, but in terms of finding the right location and spending the money on skillful contractors.

Another important aspect of building a presentable business is investing in quality equipment and supplies. This means purchasing top-of-the-line machinery for a manufacturing business, investing in high-quality ingredients for a restaurant, or buying durable and attractive furniture for a retail store. Choosing the right equipment and supplies can improve your business's appearance and functionality and demonstrate a commitment to quality and professionalism.

Of course, all of these expenditures may rapidly mount up, so it's critical to plan your spending. This entails giving more importance to investments that will positively affect the development of your company than merely splurging on glitzy or pointless things. It also entails being prepared to modify as necessary in response to client feedback and business performance.

By focusing on branding, equipment and supplies, marketing and advertising, you can create a business that looks professional and appealing to potential customers, communicates your unique value, and stands out in a crowded market.

# Chapter 6

The most difficult, but perhaps the most important step of starting a medical cannabis dispensary was acquiring its license. As we have discussed previously, it took years for the State of Louisiana to legalize cannabis for medical purposes. Therefore, those longing to start the medicinal cannabis business during the early years had to go through a rigorous process to obtain a license for a dispensary.

After hiring qualified staff and building an efficient team for our medicinal cannabis business, we moved forward to acquire a license for our dispensary. We knew it was a challenging task and we understood what was waiting for us ahead. The process of acquiring a license involved several steps. There were certain requirements that need to be met before even applying for the license, let alone acquiring it.

The first step to acquiring a license for a medicinal dispensary was to appear before the board along with all your regional competitors. We were located in Region 3 and we had some pretty big, and tough competitors. Omar devised a plan that sounded pretty achievable to me. He discussed the plan and briefed me thoroughly before we started our plan of action. I agreed to his suggestion and we started working on our plan, in order to acquire the license successfully.

To execute Omar's plan properly, we prepared ourselves through role-playing sessions. I put myself in my competitors' shoes and started playing the role of our competitors. Omar, being a member of our team would try to counter our competitors' ideas through better arguments, that were backed by adequate data. We made different scenarios, in which we portrayed our competitors' edge over us in every aspect, i,e. education, experience, and financial strength. Omar would try to counter our competitors' approaches through his presentation and practical arguments. Our plan was to beat our competition on the educational side of cannabis, the experience of running a dispensary, and financial means. During some sessions, I would pin Omar down, by providing strong arguments, just to prepare him and myself for the worst. However, that technique helped Omar in preparing himself better for D-Day. After conducting several role-playing sessions, we finally managed to derive a winnable solution, which actually helped us when we present our company in front of the board.

The preparatory sessions that we conducted were not simply enough to get us a license. The board had its own requirements as well, that needed to be met by all the applicants. The board had its own financial requirements. According to those requirements, every applicant must have a pool of at least $10,000, to manage the financial expenditures of the dispensary efficiently. However, having merely $10,000 was not enough, as one had to look out for the financial strength of their competitors. Applicants did not know about the financial strength of their competitors. So, they had to keep a pool of large reserves in case, they had to compete with a financially strong competitor. When we were preparing to appear before the board, we analyzed that we need to have a reserve of at least $1,000,000, just to get to the starting point of the game. That meant a lot of money was required to obtain the license, as we had some big shots as our competitors. We somehow managed to arrange the required amount, as we didn't want to lose the chance of acquiring a license for our dream business.

The complexities of acquiring a medicinal cannabis license in Louisiana were very challenging. First, you had to navigate the state laws, which are defined in Alison Neustrom Act. The act is named after Alison Neustrom, a mother who died of pancreatic cancer in 2014, and whose wish was to legalize medical cannabis. It was due to her struggles that the state finally decided to legalize cannabis.

Secondly, the applicants had to abide by the laws of the Louisiana Board of Pharmacy. The board's functions regarding the issuing of have been described in Alison Neustrom Act. The board of pharmacy required documents that illustrate the applicant's educational background, financial strength, industry experience, and so on. In addition to the board regulations, each applicant has to prepare an excellent presentation, to beat other competitors on the day of their evaluation by the board.

Just to give the readers an idea of the whole license acquisition process, I shall describe each and every step in brief detail. The following steps must be completed to acquire a dispensary license in Louisiana.

- o   Submit an application to the Louisiana Board of Pharmacy. This application must include detailed information about the proposed dispensary, including location, ownership, and operations.

- o Pay a non-refundable application fee set by the Board of Pharmacy.
- o Provide proof of financial stability, including a business plan, financial projections, and evidence of access to funding.
- o Provide documentation of compliance with all local zoning and land use regulations.
- o Submit fingerprints and undergo a criminal background check.
- o Provide evidence of compliance with all applicable state and federal laws and regulations.
- o Successfully completed an on-site inspection of the dispensary by the Board of Pharmacy.
- o Obtain a certificate of occupancy from the local building department.
- o Receive a license from the Louisiana Board of Pharmacy, which must be renewed annually.[4]

Anyways, so we prepared ourselves for our big day and tried to cover our all bases before the day of evaluation. We made our presentation by focusing on the educational and experienced side of our organization. Our presentation team consisted of Omar and our pharmacist, who had over thirty years of experience in pharmacy operations. Omar, on the other hand, had a vast entrepreneurial experience, that spanned over two decades. That perfect fusion of operational and entrepreneurial experience helped us in preparing a

---

[4] January 26, 2023, How to Open a Dispensary in Louisiana, Indica Online, Retrieved From: https://indicaonline.com/blog/how-to-open-a-dispensary-in-louisiana/

perfect presentation for the board members of the Louisiana Pharmacy Board.

On the day of the presentation, Omar represented us and briefed the board members about our business in complete detail. He was, of course, accompanied by our pharmacist. Omar explained our company's vision to the board members and convinced them why we would be able to achieve our vision. He described our entrepreneurial journey and explained the struggles, that we had gone through during the past years. Omar made such a great presentation that it literally made the board members walk through our journey. Our pharmacist's presence was the cherry on top, as his experience compelled the board members to take us as serious contenders for the license.

After our presentation, we could see that board members were more than impressed with our company. They all appreciated how good we did our homework before the presentation. They also praised us for our struggles throughout our business years and appreciated us for not giving up on our dreams. Although we expected a positive response from the board, we were simply astonished by the way they had appreciated our efforts. It was simply amazing!

After we were finished with our presentation, we left with the hope, that we would be awarded a license to dispense medicinal cannabis. The board's reaction raised our expectations. We felt we were a step closer to acquiring the license, as soon as we left the Pharmacy Board's building. However, we had never imagined that we would be regarded that highly by the state's board of pharmacy. We heard that we had one the best presentations. We were notified through an email, only a week after our presentation that we were awarded the license.

I still remember that day precisely. Omar informed me about the email, shouting in happiness as if he had found El Dorado, the lost city of gold. My reaction was not different from Omar's. I was on cloud nine!

We received our license three months after the day of the presentation, although we were notified a week after the presentation. However, I would say that it was worth waiting. When Omar told me that we have got the license, I felt as if my eyes were teary. The tears of joy were rolling down my face, as I looked at the heavens, thanking God that he had chosen us to help those who are suffering from different medical conditions. That day, I felt as if I landed in the Garden of Eden, roaming in its lush green fields, and enjoying its exquisite fruits and drinks. It was the day, that changed the entire course of my life, as on that day, I was legally certified to pursue my long-awaited dream of dispensing medicinal cannabis. I will say that words cannot do justice to the feelings, that Omar and I had on that special day. It was a sigh of relief after everything we've been through.

I believe that we were awarded the license because we presented our goals and vision professionally. Our qualities were our professionalism and the excellent presentation in front of the board. We answered the board's questions with proper rationale, that reflected our knowledge of the subject matter. Apart from our presentation, the documents that we provided reflected our expertise and command over the business.

`The process may sound simple, but believe me, it was anything but plain and simple. We faced many challenges during this process. We prepared rigorously for the presentation and made adequate plans to counter our competitors. Thankfully, we didn't face any unexpected hurdles in the process. However, we did face challenges from our competitors. Some of the competitors did their homework precisely and I must say they shook our confidence a little. However, we managed to overcome those challenges and ultimately acquired a license. The competition with competitors made us better, as it indicated what areas we should work on in the future to make our business more profitable.

Before concluding this chapter, I would like to explain three strategies to my readers, that I utilized personally, while I was working to acquire the license. I hope these strategies will help the readers in their practical lives and will help in developing a winning mindset.

The first and most important strategy is to know the rules of the game. You can never be successful in any industry if you are unaware of how that industry works. Therefore, it is mandatory to know entirely about the industry you wish to work in. Learn about its rules, understand how it works, and plan how you can make profits while working in this industry.

Secondly, prepare yourself rigorously to win over the contracts or licenses in your field of interest. Burn the midnight oil, and spend sleepless nights, but do not lower your guard. Believe me, this will help you greatly in your practical life.

Lastly, as Sun Tzu said, know your enemy. Although, in the world of business, there are no enemies. Instead, there are competitors that you should know about precisely. Learn your competitor's strengths and weaknesses. Try to exploit their weaknesses in your favor. Remember you will never succeed unless you do not know who your competitors are. I will conclude this chapter with Sun Tzu's famous quote about knowing your enemies, which precisely explains the importance of my third point.

"If you know the enemy and know yourself, you need not fear the result of a hundred battles. If you know yourself but not the enemy, for every victory gained you will also suffer a defeat. If you know neither the enemy nor yourself, you will succumb in every battle."

**Sun Tzu, The Art of War**

# Chapter 7

Starting a business is an easy task that anyone can achieve. However, running it successfully is entirely different, and it requires an entrepreneur's blood and sweat. Do you know that 90% of startups fail?[5] They fail because they lose motivation or lack the strategy to scale their businesses. This stat is sufficient to prove how difficult it is to run a successful, profitable business.

During our initial years, we also faced many challenges and had our fair share of struggles. However, we kept moving, motivating ourselves that we were destined to succeed. I can proudly say that we have made it through difficulties and made our business a successful venture. This chapter will discuss how we make our medicinal cannabis dispensary business profitable.

Establishing our medical cannabis dispensary was a carefully planned journey that began with a thorough study of the state's guidelines and legislation. This critical stage verified that

---

[5] Patel, N. (2015, January 16). 90% Of Startups Fail: Here's What You Need To Know About The 10%. *Forbes*. Retrieved From: https://www.forbes.com/sites/neilpatel/2015/01/16/90-of-startups-will-fail-heres-what-you-need-to-know-about-the-10/?sh=5bbe01ad6679

our activities were legally compliant and in line with the highest levels of patient care and well-being.

After critically analyzing the state laws, the next task was to find the ideal location for a cannabis dispensary. As it could be our business's make or break point, we had to look for several factors to choose the best location for our dispensary. This included a careful examination of numerous regions and cities, influenced by variables such as closeness to our target population, accessibility, and the specific requirements of the community within the parish in which we planned to operate. Our unwavering commitment to providing a seamless and impactful patient experience guided this critical decision-making process.

Our decision-making process was led by a thorough evaluation of many crucial elements, each of which played an important role in molding the destiny of our medical cannabis dispensary. A detailed examination of the region's demand was crucial to our discussions, and it served as the foundation for our venture's feasibility.

A thorough examination of the existing demand for a medical cannabis enterprise in the region was at the heart of our research. This entailed thoroughly examining market trends, patient demographics, and the changing landscape of healthcare demands. We built a foundation that met a market need and offered the prospect of positively impacting countless lives by assessing the resonance of medical cannabis across the community.

A critical point in our discussions was the need to educate the public about the numerous benefits of medical cannabis. We understood that a thorough grasp of this therapy alternative was critical to its acceptability and incorporation into the community. To that end, we launched proactive activities such as sharing factual information, holding seminars, and engaging in open debates to illustrate the potential of medical cannabis and empower consumers to make informed decisions about their health.

These immersive workshops not only offered individuals insights into the medicinal potential of medical cannabis, but also a forum for open debates, dispelling myths, and cultivating a culture of informed decision-making. In addition to this endeavor, our strategic use of social media platforms had a far-reaching influence, allowing us to interact with a varied audience and give authoritative information that transcended barriers.

The extent of medical practitioner support in the region was also important for the success of our business. We conducted considerable outreach, interviewing doctors and medical professionals to determine their willingness to promote medicinal cannabis as a valid treatment choice. This collaborative strategy ensured that our dispensary would integrate effortlessly into the current medical ecosystem, generating a sense of trust and cooperation that would benefit our patients in the long run.

As we turned our attention to the medical community, a new problem arose, educating doctors about the complexities of medical cannabis. We were fortunate that Dr Karl Haydel Sr., a luminary in his area, embraced our purpose. His support was a critical spark that set off a chain reaction within the medical community, opening the way for widespread acceptance and support of medical cannabis recommendations. May God rest his soul in peace. We Love you, Doc!

In navigating the intricacies of marketing, another distinctive challenge emerged. Constrained by the unique nature of our business, we confronted the dilemma of not being able to employ conventional marketing avenues. Undeterred, we harnessed the influential force of word of mouth, leveraging the power of personal testimonials and experiences to organically spread awareness. This grassroots approach kindled a sense of authenticity and trust that resonated deeply within our community.

Our medical cannabis dispensary's heartbeat is our precision in our day-to-day operations, which effortlessly blends accuracy and compassion to serve our patients' requirements with utmost dedication.

Our pharmacy technician takes action after obtaining a recommendation from a medical practitioner. They carefully deliver the recommendation to our professional pharmacist, who plays the critical function of preparing the required prescription. This professional collaboration guarantees that each prescription is filled with unmatched precision, demonstrating our dedication to providing safe and effective therapy.

When patients require assistance regarding their prescriptions, our pharmacist assists them with all the information they require. A face-to-face consultation follows, in which the patient and pharmacist engage in a discussion where patients can ask as many questions about medicinal cannabis as they want. This close encounter becomes a cornerstone of empowerment, as patients are equipped not just with a prescription but also with a deep awareness of the subtleties of their drug.

Managing a medicinal cannabis dispensary efficiently is vital as far as the sustainability of a business is concerned. We manage inventory, sales, and customer service through a state-run POS system. The system records every transaction, guaranteeing that our shelves are filled with the products our customers want.

To market our business, we chose a different path; we utilized the limitless potential of social media to promote medicinal cannabis. Social media became the canvas for our brand's tale, with each post and interaction creating a narrative of education, empowerment, and enlightenment. This allowed us to transcend the constraints imposed by traditional marketing, as we could not market our business like normal businesses.

The regulatory framework shaped the boundaries of our product procurement, as we were allowed to procure products from only two state-approved suppliers. It was written in the law, and we could not do anything about it. However, this exclusive supply chain was created to ensure the compliance of medicinal cannabis providers. Moreover, we could not conduct QA on the procured product as it was not allowed per the state's laws. The catch was that we had to give confidence to the public about the product we were offering. I can proudly say that we did that successfully.

We took steps to ensure we stored our medical cannabis in a secured, state-approved location. Our building met all state regulatory laws, and third, we made sure all customers were approved to get medicinal cannabis by their Doctor.

As guardians of a greater purpose, we took on a critical responsibility; ensuring that people seeking our services were deserving of medicinal cannabis. We verify that every customer is prescribed by a genuine, practicing physician. This validation procedure is more than simply a policy; it demonstrates our commitment to prioritizing the well-being of our community. We honored the purity of our goal by ensuring that every individual was recommended medicinal cannabis by a trained doctor, offering care only to those whose medical condition required it.

Our vigilance expanded beyond the walls of our dispensary, crossing. We took on the responsibility of remaining current on every new legislation regarding medicinal cannabis. We took on the role of watchful observers with each state legislative session, closely studying every detail, amendment, and change that built the legal fabric of medical cannabis. This unwavering dedication guaranteed that we navigated the legal waters with a firm hand, always ready to adapt and match our activities with the growing legal environment.

We shaped our product offers not only based on the needs of our patients but also on a keen awareness of cost dynamics. We were able to achieve a careful balance between offering effective therapies and minimizing expenditures. This created our brand loyalty as customers understood that we provide pocket-friendly solutions to their medicinal cannabis needs.

We also paid great attention to providing the best customer service to our customers. From the moment we received our license, we were directed by an unbreakable beacon, a steadfast dedication to providing nothing less than five-star customer service. This vow became the pulse that inspired every aspect of our business, an unwritten bargain we upheld with every customer who stepped through our doors. Every transaction, whether at the counter or through digital means, exemplified our commitment to exceeding expectations and turning the ordinary into the extraordinary.

This can be verified through a simple Google search. A quick Google search will show you several testimonials, each a sincere tribute to the friendships we've formed and the influence we've had. The clients' positive feedback is a source of our immense pride, serving as a live witness to our unwavering quest for excellence.

Our journey to success has not been without daunting challenges. We had our fair share of trials that mainly rose because of the federal status of cannabis. Despite its growing acceptability and therapeutic promise, cannabis' federal classification as a Schedule I narcotic casts a shadow over our activities, imposing limits that are sometimes very discouraging. However, we managed to make a good business despite all those challenges. Like all Entrepreneurs, I love a good challenge because it's not the money; it's the thrill of making a business from nothing. That's what gets me excited.

When we started our company, the concept of collaboration was non-existent in our industry. Our company started as a sole venture inspired by a firm belief in the transforming power of medical cannabis. However, during this early stage, our most significant collaboration was formed within the folds of an association that brought us together with other dispensary owners.

Our collaborative ethos was at the heart of our alliance, a dedication to combining our knowledge, ideas, and experiences to benefit people who sought our advice. We went on a journey of collective learning, accepting each other's viewpoints and reinforcing our awareness of the different needs of our clients, united by the joint aim of alleviating suffering and cultivating well-being.

We created an ecosystem of support through this dynamic interchange of ideas, where obstacles were solved with creative solutions, and triumphs were celebrated as communal accomplishments. The association served as a center for developing novel initiatives, influenced by the voices that contributed to its collective expertise.

We have created a framework that encapsulates our core principles and leads our way toward success by forming the pillars of our company's operating philosophy. The primary idea of first-rate customer service is at the center of our approach.

Customer service, our first pillar, is more than just a transactional element; it is a story of care, empathy, and unshakable dedication. We have created a paradise in which everyone who walks through the doors of Green Leaf Dispensary is greeted with love and respect, embodying the golden rule; treat others as we would like. This notion pervades every conversation, advice, and encounter, establishing the foundation of a memorable and meaningful customer journey.

Our second pillar, community outreach, and service, exemplifies our cooperative relationship with the communities we serve. We engage as active contributors outside our walls, integrating ourselves into the fabric of the towns we call home. Our outreach programs, precisely designed to meet pressing needs, are an extension of our commitment to supporting well-being and improving lives beyond medical cannabis.

Our third guiding beacon is the basis of trust with the medical community. Doctors' commitment is gained and nurtured through a deep collaboration founded on mutual respect and shared goals. Medical practitioners are vital partners and collaborators in our mission to improve patient care. We transcend the traditional boundaries of business partnerships by building an environment of open communication, constant education, and steadfast support, forming bonds that transcend transactions and contribute to better patient outcomes.

Fourth on our path is an uncompromising commitment to product quality. Our products are more than just commodities; they are manifestations of our commitment to rigorous sourcing, approvals, and validation. Every product on our shelves demonstrates our unwavering dedication to patient safety, efficacy, and well-being.

I'd like to share two fundamental concepts that have influenced my experience as an entrepreneur. These ideas, formed by experience and a dedication to excellence, serve as beacons of light for those seeking to navigate the volatile terrain of business with intelligence and grace.

The first pearl of wisdom is an uncompromising commitment to putting customers at the center of your business. Customers are more than just transactions in the active business environment; they are the pulsating force that can breathe life into your business. Nurture this relationship with extreme caution, as it has the transforming capacity to shape your path. A satisfied customer is more than simply a one-time purchase; it is evidence of your commitment to their well-being, creating a ripple effect beyond the confines of a single interaction.

Customer-centricity is more than a phrase; it is a firm commitment to creating memorable experiences. Recognize their requirements, anticipate their aspirations, and exceed their expectations. The image you leave on a customer echoes far and wide in an environment that relies on word-of-mouth and digital connectedness, becoming a beacon that pulls others to your fold.

The second pearl of wisdom is an ethics of humane treatment, not only for your customers but also for those who bring your vision to life, your staff. In a world where information travels at the speed of light, how you treat your team becomes a story that spreads throughout the community. Create an environment of respect, collaboration, and empowerment for your staff, as their well-being is an investment in your company's long-term heritage.

Extend the same attention to your staff as you do to provide excellent client experiences. A happy and engaged staff becomes brand ambassadors, promoting your business to every nook and corner through word of mouth. The culture you cultivate is a mirror in which your beliefs are reflected to the rest of the world, a culture that resonates with sincerity, compassion, and a true dedication to mutual progress. You create a story of trust, respect, and mutual benefit that crosses boundaries, enriches lives, and exemplifies the power of ethical entrepreneurship by prioritizing customers and treating employees as valued partners.

# Chapter 8

In entrepreneurship, the road from conception to realization, from idea to triumph, is a difficult trip marked by several twists and turns. Every business starts with a desire, an aim driven by passion, determination, and the confidence that success is attainable. However, this path is indeed plagued with stumbling blocks, and the road to success is frequently filled with disappointments and uncertainties.

Many people associate starting and running a successful business with risky ventures that could lead them to sleepless nights and restless days. However, such people do not know that running a successful business requires unwavering determination, a readiness to learn from mistakes, and the courage to carry on, despite facing unimaginable difficulties. A business success story consists of chapters describing the value of tenacity, adaptation, and unflinching dedication to a mission.

In this chapter, I shall discuss my personal experiences of how I managed to run my business successfully and how I converted my business into a brand. Though my journey to success was pretty challenging, I realized that it was worth the struggle when I ultimately bore the fruits of my hard work. So, I invite you to witness the challenges and strategies of running a successful business through the lens of my experiences.

We went on a quest to build on our strengths in servicing our local region and community when we set out to extend our brand. We understood our strengths and weaknesses and exploited them precisely to make our business successful. We utilized different strategies at the start of our business. Some of the strategies yielded results, while some went futile.

We kept the tactics and ideas that worked like a precious treasure. These were the foundations of our expansion, the pillars on which our brand stood tall. On the other hand, we weren't hesitant to discard what didn't work. We acknowledged that clinging to ineffective initiatives was like carrying extra baggage on a mountain trail. We acknowledged the significance of agility, the art of discarding the extra baggage to rise higher. We learned, modified, and kept moving forward by adopting fresh approaches to our mistakes and errors.

Apart from following different strategies, we also followed a set of principles that assisted us in executing our strategies according to the requirements of the business. Firstly, we were steadfast in our view that the customer is supreme. We believed in the phrase, the customer keeps the lights on. We knew that our customers could select where they spent their hard-earned money. With this in mind, we followed a customer-centric attitude, placing their wants and requirements at the forefront of all decisions. We made customer satisfaction our top priority and successfully managed to stick to that principle.

Our second pillar was an uncompromising dedication to the highest quality and standards. We had no space for compromise regarding the quality of our products because of the severe regulations of our state laws. Each item that entered our inventory bore the weight of our commitment to excellence. It wasn't just about compliance; it was about a higher standard, a dedication to giving our customers nothing but the finest.

The third component of our plan was our determination to maintain market-competitive prices of our products. We knew the significance of balance because affordability was a pillar of accessibility. We worked hard to ensure that our offers were of high quality and good value. Our pricing plan demonstrated our dedication to serving our community by ensuring that the benefits of our products were accessible to everybody.

These three principles constituted the foundation of our success. They were more than just strategies; they defined us and how we worked.

## Learning How to Scale Your Business

Suppose you are an entrepreneur with aspirations of scaling your business. In that case, you must learn from the experiences of successful business persons. Remember, their experiences can guide you to navigate the challenging waters of entrepreneurship. If you ask me for advice about scaling a business, I will say you focus on the following factors,

Before you even think about scaling, ensure your brand has a proven track record. This is the basis upon which everything else is built. Customers, whether loyal or potential, need to know they can rely on the quality of your product or the service you give. It is not enough to deliver once; it is also necessary to deliver consistently, time after again. Consider it a promise that you not only make but also zealously keep. Remember, your brand's reputation is its money, and an established track record is the gold standard.

Location is another important factor as far as scaling a business is concerned. Do not make hasty decisions without considering factors like, "Is there a population that can support your firm, and is their income level compatible with what you provide?"

Scaling is not about putting blind faith in your product. Rather, it is a calculated strategic action. Do your research, conduct market research, and ensure that the community you're entering can profit from and support your presence.

The last and one of the most important factors is marketing. Try to personalize your message to attract the masses whom you are targeting. Your marketing efforts should be comprehensive and distinctive, reflecting the special theme of the market you're entering. Consider it a discussion, not a monologue. Understand the needs and demands of the community, its culture, and values, and incorporate these insights into your marketing. Be a storyteller rather than a salesperson. Your brand should become a trusted companion in the journey of the people you want to serve.

So, for all entrepreneurs planning to expand, keep these advises in mind: create a dazzling track record, pick your battleground wisely, and tell your narrative in a way that speaks to the hearts and minds of the group you want to serve.

## Evolution of Our Products

Since our humble beginnings, the evolution of our product offerings has been nothing short of astounding. It demonstrates the power of listening, changing, and, most importantly, providing the people exactly what they want. Our product line was very different when we initially started out. We began with a modest range of products. However, as we set out on our brand-building journey, we stuck to a golden rule, which is basically the rule of thumb for every business, 'give the public what they want.' We've always believed that if you align your offers with the desires of your audience, you'll be on the right track. If you ignore it, the tide will quickly shift against you.

As a result, we formed alliances with vendors who shared our objectives. They were more than just suppliers; they were players in the big game of gratifying client wishes. They listened to the market's pulse and created items that were not simply sought but craved.

Today, our product line offers our customers a wide range of products. We offer a variety of options that cater to every palate, from gummies that titillate the taste senses to the finest flowers; we provide everything. We offer Flower, Pre-Rolls, Disposable Vape Pens, Vape Cartridges, PAX Vape Pods, Extracts, Edibles, Tinctures, Topicals, Gear, and Vapes.

You may wonder what sets us apart from other dispensaries because every other dispensary provides these products. The answer to this question is that our dedication to quality, expertise, and service sets us apart. Our selection is more than simply a catalog; it is a carefully picked collection that shows our commitment to fulfilling the different requirements of our community. It's about giving experiences, not just things, and making each visit to our dispensary a journey of exploration, comfort, and fulfillment.

## Importance of The Team in A Successful Business

Our amazing staff of qualified Pharmacist Techs and Pharmacists plays a significant role in making our business successful. They are the unsung heroes and the wise pillars of our organization.

Remember, It's not only about the products you sell; it's also about the people who make it all happen. Our path to success took an invaluable turn when I realized that a staff invested in my company's success was like a precious treasure for my business.

Our Pharmacists and Pharmacist Techs are more than just employees; they are ardent supporters of our purpose. Their knowledge extends beyond pill counting and prescription dispensing. They are aware of the complexities of patient care, the importance of medicinal cannabis, and the value of empathy in the healing process.

However, apart from their understanding of medicinal cannabis, their constant commitment to our company's success truly sets them apart. It's a principle I've grown to value, 'If one succeeds, we all succeed.' This isn't simply a slogan; it's the core of our workplace culture. It's the realization that when every member of our team is motivated by a common purpose, magic happens.

## Importance of Increasing People in Your Team

Entrepreneurs have to maintain a delicate balance to sustain their business, a balance between growth and preserving their brand identity. It's a lesson that came to me through experience, and it's one that I hold dear because it holds the key to sustaining the very essence of your business.

Suppose you created your brand from the ground up. It's more than simply a name; it's a promise to give nothing less than the best. It's more than just a label; it's become a standard that your customers have grown to anticipate. It's your brand identity, and it's invaluable.

However, as your company grows, there's often a tendency to bring on more people, and this isn't always a terrible thing; in fact, it's often a necessary stage in the growing process. However, extreme caution is required.

It is correct that adding new team members means adding new viewpoints, talent, and hands to the mix. It may broaden your vision, energize your company, and prepare you for the great scaling stage. However, remember it must be done while keeping the brand's identity in mind.

New team members should not dilute your dedication to greatness; rather, they should intensify it. They should be torchbearers for your brand values and custodians of your consumer promise. Every new team member should be a protector of your brand's DNA, someone who understands and preserves the reputation you've established.

So, when you go on your journey of expansion, keep this in mind: expanding your team can be a catalyst for greatness, but it should always be in the service of improving, not eroding your brand identity. Your brand is your legacy, your promise to customers, and the reason they select you. It's your guide, and sustaining it ensures that you keep your company's essence intact as you develop.

## Piece of Advice for the Readers

The first piece of advice I would give to aspiring entrepreneurs is to always think big. Entrepreneurship is not for the faint of heart; it requires optimists, dreamers, and brave visionaries. It's about reaching for the stars because what do you have to lose when beginning from scratch?

I recall the early days of my own firm when all I had was a dream and hope. I was broke, with bills hanging like storm clouds on the horizon, yet I held to my faith. That steadfast belief that, against all odds, I could make my vision a reality kept me going.

After keeping faith in yourself, look for ways to brand your business. Branding is an essential component of your entrepreneurial DNA. Begin branding as soon as your company takes its first steps. Your brand is more than a logo or a name; it's a promise to your customers. When you brand your company from the beginning, you lay the groundwork for future success. You tell the world you are present, devoted, and serious about your work.

However, branding alone is insufficient. Entrepreneurs are distinguished by their faith and their unwavering trust in their mission. It is the courage to aim high and pursue aspirations even when the odds are stacked against you. When you start with nothing, you have the flexibility to dream big, take chances, and design your own path.

So, for all aspiring entrepreneurs, remember to think big, brand early, and keep your faith. Your journey may begin modestly, but with vision, determination, and a drive to shoot for the heavens, you may create a success story beyond your wildest expectations. It's not about what you stand to lose; it's about what you stand to gain.

# Chapter 9

Starting a business is easy; scaling your business requires blood and sweat. It is like setting the sails toward new horizons. A minor mistake can cost you your hard work and investment. This chapter will discuss the lessons I learned while scaling our business. I shall try to enlighten the readers on why scaling and growth are important for businesses and how they can grow their businesses.

To begin, consider your expansion in the same way as you would choose a home. Look for a city or location that resonates with the mission and vision of your company. It's not just about selecting the right location; it's about finding a place where your brand can grow and effortlessly penetrate into every household in the community. Always consider your business location as the magnifying glass of your business' vision.

The second factor to consider before scaling your business is your target market. Conduct thorough research around questions like, "Is there a market for your services or products in this new industry?" Always conduct extensive market research to understand the needs and desires of the community you are going to join. Your business is not only about money; it is about becoming a part of the daily lives of the people you want to help.

Trust me, if you follow the first two steps with dedication, things will turn around. Suppose you manage to choose the right location and hit the right chords of your target market. In that case, your business will sustain, and you will automatically feel the need for scaling.

Scaling allows you to go beyond matching your previous accomplishments and establish a new standard of excellence. It is more than just making money. It is about cultivating fertile ground for your brand to take root and grow into a powerful tree with a broad shade of impact. It is the scaling that gives your company life.

In today's competitive business environment, scaling has become necessary for any business. It is not a choice anymore. Staying static in the dynamic business ecosystem is equivalent to withering. Your firm may wither if you do not scale and seek out new markets. It's the battle between the competitors. Only the fittest will survive this battle. The choice is yours: either adapt and thrive or remain static and face decline.

## Why Growth is Important

Growth is the most important part of any business, defining its success and profitability. To introduce and establish your brand in new cities and communities, growth is required. Establishing your brand in new places is more than just marketing it on billboards; it's about bringing your business' vision into the lives of new communities.

Your inspirations are the driving force behind the growth of your business. Scaling becomes a necessity rather than a choice when you have big business ambitions. Your inspiration helps your brand resonate through new neighborhoods, transcend state lines, and become a household name in various communities. In short, your inspiration motivates you to grow your business and take it to new heights.

Remember, growth is the essence of leaving your mark on the world. It's about telling your brand story to new places and new communities. As you grow and expand, you establish a legacy that transcends borders and connects with people from different backgrounds.

Now, you might be wondering how to achieve growth and profitability in your businesses. Remember, the key to growth and successful expansion is research. It's similar to looking at a map before embarking on a cross-country road trip. All you need to do is understand the subtleties of the new territory and ensure that your brand's persona will echo just as powerfully in the new environments as it has been echoing for the past several years.

Once you are done with your business expansion, analyze its success through profitability. Profitability is the perfect yardstick to measure the success of your business. It tells you if you're on the right track. If your company has thrived throughout the years, weathering storms and emerging stronger, you're not just working; you've discovered a formula that works.

## My Principles: The Force Behind My Business Growth

Our scaling adventure taught us an important lesson. Before venturing into new territory, consider what makes your wheel unique, what makes it not just a part of the community but the primary attraction. A business' growth is not about recreating the wheel; it's about putting your own twist on it. It's about giving your wheel a new touch, something that sets it apart from the crowd.

Scaling fundamentally means offering your wheel to a new audience. They have seen wheels and ridden in them before, so why should yours be the one they remember? So, before venturing into new markets, consider what makes your wheel turn heads. Consider the factors like, "Is it the high quality of your products? Unrivaled client service? How have you adapted your brand to fit the unique feel of each community?"

Maybe it's a mix of these, or maybe there's a hidden element that only your wheel has. The goal is to recognize, appreciate, and use it as a guide to navigate the untapped territories. So, as you prepare to scale, bring more than just a wheel; bring a spectacle, an experience that will entice everyone to take a ride on what you're giving. It's not just about having a wheel; it's about having the wheel that everyone wants to spin.

Apart from market research and product design, three principles served as anchors for my business. These three principles are faith, discipline, and a determined spirit.

The first is faith, the calm but steadfast belief that everything has a grand design. It's like sailing through stormy seas, knowing the shore is within reach. My path was about more than just earnings and losses; it was about believing that each stride forward, no matter how uncertain, was a step toward achieving a goal.

Discipline is one of the most important principles that an entrepreneur requires. The day-in, day-out dedication to the grind and the little but persistent activities pave the way to success. It is like watering the seeds of your business with your sweat and blood.

Then there's determination, the fire in the belly, the refusal to settle for anything less than being the best at what you have been given the opportunity to achieve. When everyone else is taking a rest, you go the additional mile. My quest was about more than just starting a company; it was about leaving a legacy and being known not for the business that I started but for the quality of products I introduced at pocket-friendly prices.

These ideals were more than words; they served as my guide and helped me achieve whatever I have achieved to this day. When the storms came and doubts began to creep in, faith told me to keep sailing. Discipline reminded me to keep watering the seeds when the daily grind became boring. And when the road seemed difficult, resolve said, "You're here to be the best." So, to all aspiring entrepreneurs, consider these three companions while you enter the competitive business arena.: faith, discipline, and determination.

## Future Prospects for My Medicinal Cannabis Business

My brother and I were inspired by working in healthcare and witnessing firsthand the toll diseases have on people. We wanted to do something about the healing of the people. So, we decided to start a new dispensary. Our aim in starting the medicinal cannabis dispensary at a second location was to make a difference in people's lives.

Apart from empathy, we also considered the financial aspects of the medicinal cannabis market. The figures and the trends spoke a language that we could understand. However, I will say it again: it wasn't just about making money (though that was one reason); it was about entering a market that could combine financial success with the noble aim of improving people's health.

So, opening another dispensary was more than just a commercial decision; it was a strategic step toward a larger goal. It's about spreading the healing power of cannabis to more people and creating an environment where wellness isn't simply a destination but a journey.

## Process to Open Another Dispensary

We followed the same steps to open another dispensary we took to open our first one.

Our first step was to identify the ideal location. We considered different sites in our region, just like the first time, evaluating neighborhoods, footfall, and sentiments. Many people misunderstand the meaning of finding an ideal location for a business. An ideal location is not the one that is located in the heart of any city. Instead, finding an ideal location means locating a spot that connects with the sentiments of the community you are targeting. So, after a thorough research, we finally identified an ideal location for our second dispensary.

The next step, of course, was obtaining a license. It's not the most exciting aspect of the process, but it's vital. We obtained the various licenses required to operate a medicinal cannabis dispensary. Since we already knew the steps to obtain the license, we didn't face many difficulties acquiring one for our second dispensary.

The third and the last step was hiring the architect. Hiring someone who knows engineers and contractors is like getting half the job done. We hired one such architect, who looked after the complete construction and renovation process.

Now, you may wonder whether we faced any difficulties in opening our second dispensary. Let me tell you, we did not face any difficulties while opening our second dispensary, not in terms of surprises or setbacks, at least. It was because we had already poured our hearts, sweat, and tears into our first site. We were well-versed in the game's rules and complexities.

## My Insights for the Readers

Always be prepared to expand your business. It's like packing your bag and going on a trip. If your business is doing well and yielding good profits, then the first thing you should consider is to scale it to new heights. You may ask why you need to scale your business when it's already doing fine. The answer is that scaling is the art of celebrating current accomplishments and creating a plan for the future.

However, always keep in mind that nothing lasts forever. Do not consider this sentence to be a prediction. Rather, consider it a reminder that the business arena is as fluid as the seasons. Therefore, always prepare yourself for the rainy days. Maybe that day will come, maybe it won't, but either way, you will be prepared.

So, to young entrepreneurs, embrace your company's profitability, but don't get too comfortable. Always have future goals and plans in the back of your mind. It's not about fear of the unknown; it's about looking forward to the success of your business. Always keep an eye on the horizon because the true beauty of business isn't just in the ascent; it's also about tackling the challenges that come your way. Remember, true entrepreneurs always plan for the future. They create their own stories and build their own dreams. Their farsightedness distinguishes them from ordinary people. They can see beyond the horizon and predict future turbulences in business environments.

# Chapter 10

My entrepreneurial journey is nothing less than a wild, adventurous roller-coaster ride. I had fallen into debacles, but I rose every time like a true champion. My redemption after every debacle was the result of my faith and discipline in life.

I was a millionaire at the young age of 21, with the world at my feet. Life was a celebration, and I was the center of it. But, as fate would have it, the bright life turned into a haunting, dark one when I reached 25. I found myself facing the opposite side of success, the one marked by failures, losses, and going bankrupt.

It was the most testing time of my life, and it could lead me anywhere. I could have lost my hopes, and my entrepreneurial dreams might have withered away by the raging storms of my life. However, during those dark times, faith and discipline helped to rise above the challenges and face them with dignity. I never wavered nor questioned the Creator. Instead, I clung to my faith like it was a lifeline. I knew that the Creator was testing me with hardships and that he had planned something better for me in the future.

I maintained my discipline even during the darkest periods. It was the most challenging period of my life, but I am grateful to the Creator, who gave me the strength to endure those hardships.

I knew that if I stayed true to my ideals and kept moving forward with purpose, my rainy days would be over.

Seven years in the financial wilderness was a test of endurance and faith. However, after all the agonies and pains, the Creator brought me out of those challenges and provided me with a new chance to restart my entrepreneurial life.

## Lawsuit: How Faith Helped Me in Coming Out of the Most Terrible Phase of My Life

I made my first million when I was just twenty-one. At that time, I decided to start a business that seemed the next big thing. As soon as I became a 'millionaire,' I co-founded a pecan candy company with my cousin. I won't lie; I felt unstoppable. It was that point in life when you believe you're on a roll and that every step you make is destined for success. During that time, I thought I could transform dust into gold by merely touching it.

Life, on the other hand, had different ideas for me. My crowning achievement, the candy company, went bankrupt. Imagine your shock and disbelief when something you thought was impenetrable crumbled right before you. To make things worse, my cousin sued me for the failure of the business. It was the most painful experience as I was sued by my business partner, who was my cousin as well. It was a blow to the ego, a humbling experience I hadn't seen coming.

Now, looking back on it, I realize it was a turning point in my life, a divine signal that redirected my journey. The lawsuit and the failures did not deter me from my inspiration; rather, they became my stepping stones. They fortified my faith, strengthened my resolve, and taught me the invaluable lesson of humility. There were battles ahead, and I needed intangible weapons for those battles: faith, humility, and the knowledge that comes from admitting you are not in control of everything in your life.

## Importance of Faith

For those aspiring entrepreneurs who want to start their own business, remember faith and willpower is the most crucial element of any business. Suppose you have a goal and a burning desire to make it a reality. In that case, these two principles will help you succeed even if you do not have abundant financial resources or any contacts in the industry. Your willpower is the attitude that motivates you to start, even from meager financial resources. It encourages you to take the first step. Always try to strengthen your faith in the Creator. Stay humble in the success and face the failures with dignity.

Moreover, try to learn from your problems; treat them as your guides in life. You can also learn from my experiences. I didn't allow my failures to become hurdles in the way of success. Rather, I treated them as divine interventions that were there to make me stronger and help me succeed in life. Every failure taught me something, and believe me, the lessons I learned from those failures were priceless. So, always keep in mind that starting a business is not just about the balance sheets and marketing strategies; it's about the intangibles, faith, willpower, humility, and wisdom that come after encountering failures in life.

## How Discipline and Consistency Helped Me in My Medicinal Cannabis Venture?

My discipline played an integral part when I started my cannabis dispensary business. I started my business with my brother. We both knew each other's natures, and we both understood each other's strengths and weaknesses. Growing up together had been a blessing, but we had learned the skill of keeping family and business separate.

So, we started the business with a strong strategy. Knowing each other and understanding each other's strengths, we planned to expand our business within the first six months. We knew what we needed to do, and we understood the market dynamics. However, due to circumstances beyond our control, it took us five years to reach our milestone.

During that time, discipline played a crucial role in my life. It motivated me to keep moving toward my goal, regardless of how difficult the circumstances were. Discipline became my constant companion during those challenging five years. Even when the rewards were slow to come, it was the force that kept me doing the things that drew attention to our dispensary.

My discipline and perseverance eventually paid off. Everything we did to draw attention to the dispensary, as well as the regularity we maintained, paid off. Our patience transformed into victory. We finally managed to yield profits from our cannabis dispensary.

## Piece of Advice for the Readers

To my readers, always keep the faith and be disciplined in life. Discipline is your road map, the guidance that keeps you on track. These are not hollow words; rather, I have lived up to these words and have yielded rewards by following these principles. Faith and discipline have been my collaborators in the cannabis industry. They helped me swim against the strong waves of uncertainty.

So, dear readers, when you enter the world of entrepreneurship, have faith and discipline. Do not lose your grip on these principles even for a second. Trust me, if you stay rooted in these, you will attract success just like the magnet attracts iron.

Lastly, I would like to thank you all for reading my book. I hope you learned a lot about business starting strategy in the cannabis industry. Good luck for starting your business. Remember this advice when venturing into the cannabis market or any other endeavor: faith and discipline are your guides. Good luck, fellow doers and dreamers. If you want to learn more about me and my business, read my next book, "I am on Fire." Until then, may your dreams be big, your faith be firm, and your discipline be unwavering

www.ingramcontent.com/pod-product-compliance
Lightning Source LLC
Chambersburg PA
CBHW072334290526
45794CB00002B/867